THE ART OF FOREPLAY

FOREPLAY IDEAS THAT WOULD DRIVE ANY WOMAN WILD

ANTHONY EKANEM

Made with ♥ on the Notion Press Platform
www.notionpress.com

Contents

Preface

The purpose of this book is to teach you how to put a woman in the mood for sex, so she will desire to have sex with you over and again. If you are a man who has difficulty connecting with your woman sexually, this book will help you to overcome that.

Foreplay is one thing all women cannot get enough of. Women are very emotional, and that is why they like, enjoy and always desire foreplay. So, your duty as a man is to give your woman what she wants. And she will respond by giving you what you want also. Unlike men, women do not easily get aroused sexually. This is because their bodies need some help to warm up, and to produce the required lubrication for enjoyable sex. Women's emotions also require that they feel a sense of closeness and mutual respect with their partners. You can achieve all of this through foreplay, which will also help your partner feel desired by you.

If you just want to jump on your partner and have sex with her without adequately preparing her body for it, she will feel like a sex object that you merely want to use to satisfy yourself. Now, every woman is different, and some of them might be able to get right into sex without foreplay. The odds, however, are that your woman will need to get wet sufficiently first before you too can enjoy the sex.

The ART of Foreplay

Foreplay is important to every woman when it comes to sexual intercourse. I have discovered as well that a woman's body was made up just for that. The woman has a lot of erogenous zones on her body that you can stimulate to arouse her sexually. Of all the erogenous zones, however, the most important one is her brain. That is why women feel more sense of romance when they are with someone they like. This tells you that foreplay should always start from that most important part of the woman's body, which is her brain.

We will be discussing the following areas of foreplay in this book:

1. Mental Foreplay
2. Stimulating Her Erogenous Zones
3. Kissing

CHAPTER ONE

Mental Foreplay

Foreplay should not start from the bedroom. Once you are already in a relationship, you as the man should be romantic. What I mean by that is that you should mentally alert your partner to be open to sexual ideas and talk with you. The main thing here is *anticipation*.

Anticipation

I believe that *anticipation*, *excitement*, and *tension* are some of the biggest turn-ons that a woman can feel. Women like to wonder what is coming next. They want to be surprised. They like to be waiting on the edge of their seats.

Here are a few ways to do it:

1. Say "I have a surprise for you." Then say "But I'm not going to give it to you yet. It is for later." The surprise can be anything from a piece of chocolate or a soft massage cream that you bought to rub her shoulders; it does not matter. The key is to trigger her curiosity and make her want to know what it is. You can also use your phone to send her a message as well.

1. Put a blindfold on her. Now, this is where it gets interesting. Remember that I told you I am going to

help you change the way your wife or partner sees you. Women love to be blindfolded! Don't ask, just do it. Grab a scarf out of her wardrobe (silk if you have it) and put it on her. Remember, women tend to be turned on more by their other senses. So, turning their vision off intensifies their other senses and makes them even more responsive to your touch and lovemaking.

3. When you are doing something that is turning her on, stop. This seems counter-intuitive, but it is the promised land. Men like to find what feels good and keep doing it. Women like to have what feels good taken away, so they can feel more anticipation because anticipation turns them on even more. You can also come up with your own ways to build anticipation. Tell her a story about someone that felt anticipation. Just make her anticipate what is coming next.

4. Talking to a woman during foreplay (or even sex) will stimulate her imagination, and since the best way to sex a woman is through stimulation of her brain, just picture the intense flow of orgasmic pleasure that she will begin to feel. But mind you, this is not the time to say silly things like: "what are we taking for dinner tonight?" Instead, ask questions and say something that will get her imagination working.

  i. What do you want me to do to you right now?
 ii. Do you want me to go inside here?
iii. Do you want me to lick between your thighs?

If you do not have any exciting things to say, a good idea is just for you to keep quiet.

If you can describe how you want to touch her, where and with which of your body parts, she will visualise it easily and eagerly. The point here is that if you know how to have sex with her brain (it is a major sexual organ), you can rest assured that she will be begging you to have sex with the rest of her body in due time.

CHAPTER TWO

Stimulating the Erogenous Zones

I told you that a woman's body has a lot of erogenous zones. I am now going to share the hottest zones with you and how to handle them properly.

The Erogenous Zones Are:
1. The lips
2. The Clitoris (Vagina area)
3. The Breasts
4. The Wrists
5. Her Feet
6. Her Ears
7. The Nape of Her Neck
8. Her Buttocks
9. Behind her knees
10. Inner Thighs

So, let's get into them.

Her Lips. If you know how to manipulate the woman's lips right, through kissing, licking, sucking, and biting, a kiss may lead to so much more. Use your lips, tongue, and teeth to play with her top and bottom lips and kiss her with absolute passion.

Her Breasts. There are two parts to this. Number one is handling the breast alone without touching the nipples. As I am sure this is no surprise to you, the breasts are very sexually sensitive and gentle fondling, squeezing, caressing of it is arousing. Plus, it is important to pay attention to more than just the nipples, since the woman's entire breast is packed full of nerves, especially the underside.

Use your fingertips to draw broad, slow circles, starting around the perimeter of one breast and spiralling in until you are just about at her nipple. Then use your hand to cup and lift the underside of her breast, and lick around her nipple before covering it entirely with your mouth and sucking gently. You can then move on to the nipples and caress them, lick and suck them. If the woman has big enough nipples, you can hold both gently with your thumb and middle finger and slowly rub them. If you do this right, it will make her boil with passion. When you find that there is a specific way that you are doing it that is giving her pleasure, take note of that and focus on doing more of it to arouse her the more. More on the woman's breasts later.

Her Wrists. This may not work for every woman, but it is worth trying. What you have to do to the wrists is to nuzzle and nibble them. The next time you are getting into foreplay with your woman, begin kissing and caressing her wrists and just check how impressed and excited she may become!

Her Buttocks. Many women like it when you play around with their backsides. A lot of women like gentle touching and squeezing of the buttocks.

Her Feet. Many women enjoy having their feet touched or massaged, and some enjoy having them licked or sucked. Assuming that their feet are thoroughly cleansed, women enjoy it when their men spend a good time caressing their soles, toes, and ankles. Because these zones can all be sensitive, the sensation of ticklishness can be pleasant for her.

Her Ears. Most women explode with excitement when their ears are licked, sucked, or kissed. Although blowing in their ear is acceptable, it is not what women enjoy usually. Besides the things I have already mentioned, women also like it when you whisper in their ears.

Behind Her Knees. Because of the nerve endings in the knees, you would be surprised at how excited a woman can be when you gently lick or nibble on the back of her knees. Be careful, however, not to overdo it. The area is very sensitive, and you must be careful not to make the feeling irritating by being too rough or tickling her too much.

Inside her thighs. The inside of a woman's thighs is highly sensitive to touch, stroking and licking. Like the back of the knees, the inner thighs of women also have a lot of nerve endings. Therefore, when you caress them, you will turn her on significantly. Remember not to bite them because the area is very sensitive, and doing so would only cause the woman pain, which can, in turn, cause you plenty of pain.

The Nape of her Neck. The nape is the bottom hairline in the back of the head. That is where the skull meets the neck. The top back of the head is the crown of the head.

Merely breathing on this part of the woman's body will give her goosebumps all over. So, imagine her reaction when you use your tongue or teeth to get her aroused. Use your hands too; lift her hair gently as you bring your mouth close to her neck. Then, as you drop your teeth into it, pull on her hair slightly to give that "I want you so badly" impression. This part of a woman's body is also an excellent place to start giving her that sensual massage you are famous for, and no woman can resist that.

The Clitoris. You can stimulate the clitoris by using your tongue, finger or both simultaneously. Some women like to guide their partners as to the specific amount of pressure they enjoy.

I hope you learnt from these. I am now going to tell you more about handling the breasts. This is one powerful erogenous zone that many men do not know how to handle very well.

Handling Her Breasts in a Unique Way for Maximum Pleasure

Breasts come in different shapes and sizes. Some are perky, while others are somewhat "relaxed". Some areolas (the dark skin around the nipple) are bigger than others, and even nipples themselves come in different shapes and sizes. The bottom line is that we men love breasts, and women themselves know this. That is why you see some of them showing off just to set men up. And today, you are going to learn about all the exciting things you can do with a woman's breasts that you are fortunate enough to have staring you in the face.

Introduction to "the Twins"

When it comes to breasts, all ducts lead to the nipple, which is centred in the areola. The actual breast is made up of fat and breast tissue. There is no muscle in the breasts themselves. The muscle lies underneath the breasts, covering the ribs.

There are many nerve-endings in breasts so the nipples should not be the only aspect that you pay attention to. On that note, it is time to go into details on how to play with the breasts. Women are very proud of their breasts. Not only do they show them off more than ever before, but they want you to pay attention to them during foreplay and lovemaking.

Merely taking the breasts as if they were a piece of fruit and chewing on the nipples is going to get you nowhere, fast. That is not impressive. Like with the lovemaking experiences, taking it slow is a lot better. Before you rush to the bedroom to start caressing her away, keep in mind that, although many women love it when men caress their breasts, some could find the approach too rough and annoying. Always pay attention to a woman's reaction whenever you are having sex with them.

Hands-on Approach

When the breasts are exposed and begging to be touched, work your magic by using your hands to outline the outer part of both breasts slowly and lightly. This will quickly give the woman sensations, and her nipples will become erect. Gently move your hands over them, smoothing your palms over the nipples very slightly. The idea to tease her and let her mind run wild imagining what it is going to feel like when your tongue finally comes on them.

While the woman is lying down and her body is at your disposal, kiss around the borders of her breasts. Start kissing the outline slowly with your moist lips. Another great thing you can do is squeeze her breasts together and kiss down the middle lightly. Make your way close to the nipples and breathe over them so that she can feel the warmth of what is to come. The tongue works well for licking women's breasts. The beautiful mounts are designed flawlessly so that a mouth can cover their tops.

There is a right time to get a little rougher on the breasts. But for now, use the tip of your tongue to circle the areola. Let your tongue glide over the nipples very lightly. If the woman jerks or she lets a sudden moan escape from her lips, that is because she is almost dying for you to take the nipples into your mouth, and suck and nibble away.

If the nipples are standing at erection, harden your tongue and flick them back and forth, and slowly take them into your mouth. At this point, you should begin to suck and nibble simultaneously. If the nipples are not hard, you can manipulate them by sucking them and then releasing them from your mouth while inhaling so that it creates an icy sensation.

Add Some Variety

By now, you already know how important variety is when it comes to the subject of having enjoyable sex. Use your hands to hold the breasts while you suck on them, one at a time. You don't have to squeeze or bring each nipple to your mouth. Instead, use your hands to cup them while you bring your mouth to one, and then the other. As well, do not just stick to the nipples. Lick that space between the breasts, lick right under the breasts. Do not limit yourself to the main parts. Because these other areas don't get much attention, they are likely to be sensitive to the tongue.

And if you can do more than one thing at a time, you can be working on her breasts while you have already penetrated her. You can achieve this easily when you get into the side-by-side position (facing each other). Suck on one nipple, and lightly squeeze the other with your thumb and index finger.

This will speed up the amount of time that she needs to orgasm because her whole body will be boiling with maximum pleasure. What is even better is to have the woman on top of you and place her nipples in your mouth, one at a time. Let the head of your penis tease the vagina, while you hold on to the breasts, placing each nipple into your mouth one at a time. Breasts-play should be incorporated into your entire foreplay experience, so make the breast-play an exciting situation and pay close attention to them. Let me now talk about kissing.

Kissing

Here, I won't be focusing mainly on kissing the woman in her mouth because there are other places where she wants you to kiss her. You can apply your mouth to various other parts of her body by kissing, licking, nibbling, biting, and sucking them. Wherever you touch her with your hands will most likely feel better when you stimulate it with a warm kiss. When it comes to kissing women, some of their favourite places are obvious, while others are frequently overlooked. Let me tell you the areas where your kisses can wreck a lot of havoc on her and get her to melt.

Ears

I have already told you earlier that the ears are sensitive. The ears are an often-neglected part of the body that can be the location of intense pleasure for the woman, and using your mouth is the best way to stimulate that part. Gentle nibbling on the earlobe is a reliable way to send shivers down her spine, but you should also try lightly brushing your lips against her ear, which will rouse the soft, fine hairs there creating waves of tingly pleasure.

The Back of the Neck

One of the easiest and most effective ways to get the woman in the mood for sex is to place your mouth on the back of her neck. This works exceptionally well if you take her by surprise. So, when she is in the kitchen doing dishes or working on something else, move to her quietly from behind, pack her hair to one side of her neck and gently kiss her there. She would soon forget her task and want more.

The Face

There are just a few things more personal than kissing a woman on the face. You can express your warm, fuzzy feelings for her by placing sweet, light kisses on her cheeks, forehead, jawline, or even her nose and closed eyelids. But do not lick her face. It is not sexy. Do not bite either. A woman's face should be treated with tenderness.

The Collarbone

While your woman's clothes are still on, one of the most intimate places you can lay some kisses on is the collarbone. A woman's collarbone is sexy, and your mouth on it can make her think of your mouth on other private parts of her body. So, start with kisses there before you move on to places you can't reach while she's fully clothed.

The Hips

The woman's hips are more sensitive than you may think. It could be because they are so close to the centre of the woman's physical pleasure. Whatever the reason, kissing, licking, and nibbling on a woman's hips will send currents of sensation down to her toes and up to her head. Don't neglect this place; she would like your mouth to be there.

The Breasts

Putting your mouth on a woman's breasts can be incredibly sexy but doing it wrongly can turn her off. Kissing, licking, and sucking of the breasts are all recommended, and even some gentle biting can be acceptable if you do it gently. Women's breasts are delicate, so don't forget that you must handle them appropriately. Also, remember, as I mentioned earlier on that the nipples are not the only parts that need some attention.

Use your mouth all over the breasts for maximum pleasure. Depending on the woman, there are some parts of their body that they cannot stand kissing. Once you move your mouth to a particular region and the woman becomes resistant, move your mouth away from there.

I hope all these make sense to you, as you make love to your woman.